Biblical Prescriptions For Life's Troubles

Biblical Prescriptions For Life's Troubles

Terry Stephens

J MERRILL

J Merrill Publishing, Inc.
434 Hillpine Drive
Columbus, OH 43207
www.JMerrill.pub

Library of Congress Control Number: 2023906417
ISBN-13: 978-1-954414-89-1 (Paperback)
ISBN-13: 978-1-954414-90-7 (eBook)

Book Title: Biblical Prescriptions For Life's Troubles
Author: Terry Stephens
Cover Artwork: Safeer Ahmed

Contents

Introduction

For many, today's chaos, confusion, and troubles seem to be worse than before. But any historian will tell you that none of the issues our world faces today are new. We've had war and climate issues before. We've had mass shootings and, yes, even pandemics before. So, in many ways, nothing has changed. Yet many things have changed. For example, social media has taken over our phones and technology devices. Unfortunately, for many, social media is the primary source of misinformation and critical information. As a result, many are undecided on whether to get the COVID-19 vaccine or not, and it's causing great division among the people in groups of the world.

As the kingdom endeavors to do its part in the world, it must address the issues of division running wild throughout America and the world. Some have even followed the science and advised believers to take the vaccine. I don't have an issue with those who take the vaccine; I believe it should be a personal choice. But I have an issue with people being demonized and ridiculed for not taking it. That's not the godly way of doing things. However, one thing that I have not heard a lot of is what is the biblical prescription for these issues.

Medicine is defined as the science or practice of the diagnosis, treatment, and prevention of disease or a compound or preparation used to treat or prevent disease, especially a drug or drugs taken by mouth. The word prescribe means to advise and allow the use of (a medicine or treatment) for someone, especially in writing, or recommend (a substance or action) as something beneficial or to state authoritatively that (an action or procedure) should be performed. Why is there no biblical response? Indeed, in times like these, there must be a word from the Lord. Certainly, God is not sitting by quietly and allowing all this chaos, confusion, and calamity. I believe there is a word from the Lord about these issues. What is God prescribing? What treatment or action should believers take in response to some troubles of life?

Before we dive deep into our discussion, let me clarify a myth about a particular scripture. In Job 14, you will find this scripture.

> *"Man, who is born of woman, is short of days and full of trouble. (Job 14:1)*

First, I feel it's essential to make it known that this scripture is Job's words and not God's. Job was grieving the loss of his children when this scripture was written. Many preach this text as if God said it and it was the truth. No, these are the feelings of a man who just lost all of his children and much of his wealth. It's important to highlight these context issues for proper understanding. The same goes for Job's scripture: "The Lord giveth and the Lord taketh away, blessed be the name of the Lord." This is not a declaration of the word of the Lord, but the lamentation of a hurting man.

But Jesus says in the book of John chapter 16, "I have told you these things so that in Me you may have peace. In the world, you will have tribulation (trouble). But take courage; I have overcome the world!" (John 16:33)

Introduction

When trouble arises in our lives, we remember that the fight is fixed. 2 Corinthians 4:8 says, "We are troubled on every side, yet not distressed; we are perplexed, but not in despair"; that word distressed is the Hebrew word stenochoreo. It means to be in a narrow place; to straiten, compress, cramp, to hem in. We always understand that as long as we have the Holy Spirit dwelling inside us, we are never out of options, opportunities, or possibilities.

The scriptures say that God is even more active in our lives during times of trouble. David says it like this in Psalms 46:1 God is our refuge and strength, a very present help in trouble.

The word trouble is the Hebrew word "tsarah". It means distress, tribulation, adversity, affliction, or anguish.

It is a fact that we all will experience trouble in our lives. No one is exempt from it. You can't run from it, pray it away, or cry enough to avoid it. This is what Job was discussing. He understood that this was a part of life. But he was speaking from his experience, not from inspiration from God.

Trouble is not whether you will experience it, it's recognizing where your trouble is coming from. By identifying where your trouble comes from gives you the information to diagnose what your response should be. Doctors and physicians ask questions to locate where the illness or injury is in order to properly prescribe a medicinal solution or medicinal way to ease the pain. Identifying where our trouble comes from helps us find a biblical response to our trouble.

Some would say well the response should always be to pray and I agree with that. But sometimes prayer isn't enough. It also depends on how you pray. The natural response is to pray for deliverance, but some trouble has a time stamp on it, so your prayer may need to change to help me endure this. God told Abraham the children of Israel would be in Egyptian bondage for 400 years. With this understanding, we need to discuss the different types of trouble.

Introduction

As I've studied this subject, I've discovered six types of trouble.

1. Personal internal conflict trouble
2. People trouble
3. Personal principle trouble
4. Demonic resistance trouble
5. Bad trouble that God allowed
6. Good trouble from God

> *He shall deliver thee in six troubles: yea, in seven there*
> *shall no evil touch thee.* (Job 5:19)

The first and likely most important trouble you could ever encounter is the trouble from within—the internal conflict of the mind.

> *I do not understand what I do. For what I want to do*
> *I do not do, but what I hate I do. And if I do what*
> *I do not want to do, I agree that the law is*
> *good. As it is, it is no longer I myself who do it,*
> *but it is sin living in me. For I know that good*
> *itself does not dwell in me, that is, in my sinful*
> *nature. For I have the desire to do what is good,*
> *but I cannot carry it out. For I do not do the good*
> *I want to do, but the evil I do not want to do—this*
> *I keep on doing. Now if I do what I do not want*
> *to do, it is no longer I who do it, but it is sin living*
> *in me that does it. So I find this law at*
> *work: Although I want to do good, evil is right*
> *there with me. For in my inner being I delight in*
> *God's law; but I see another law at work in me,*
> *waging war against the law of my mind and*
> *making me a prisoner of the law of sin at work*
> *within me. What a wretched man I am! Who will*
> *rescue me from this body that is subject to*

> *death? Thanks be to God, who delivers me*
> *through Jesus Christ our Lord! So then, I myself*
> *in my mind am a slave to God's law, but in my*
> *sinful nature a slave to the law of sin. (Romans*
> *7:15-25 NIV)*

The internal conflict in our nature is the most significant among all other troubles. When we can overcome this conflict between our divine and natural natures, we are empowered to deal with all other troubles. One thing about this trouble is that we never truly overcome it until either death or the coming of Christ. When people give their life to Christ, their spirit is saved, not their flesh. The flesh will still crave all the ungodly things it did before being saved. That appetite to fulfill the lust of the flesh will always be active in a person's life. However, it can be overcome through sanctification. This is a never-ending fight, but thankfully we haven't been left hopeless, helpless, or victims. God has equipped every believer with the power to overcome the flesh nature with the Holy Spirit.

> *But ye shall receive power, after that the Holy Ghost is*
> *come upon you: and ye shall be witnesses unto me*
> *both in Jerusalem, and in all Judaea, and in*
> *Samaria, and unto the uttermost part of the earth.*
> *(Acts 1:8 KJV)*

This power of the Holy Spirit is the most vital Kingdom equipment you will ever receive. It is the DNA of Christ inside of you, leading and guiding you into all truth. If allowed to lead, this spirit will cause you to live and operate like Jesus.

> *For as many as are led by the Spirit of God, they are*
> *the sons of God. (Romans 8:14 KJV)*

> *But as many as received him, to them gave he power to*

become the sons of God, even to them that believe
on his name: (John 1:12 KJV)

This Holy Spirit was given to us for this trouble and others, to fight the lust of the flesh.

This I say then, Walk in the spirit, and ye shall not
fulfil the lust of the flesh. (Galatians 5:16 KJV)

Friends, let me tell you, walking in the spirit is no 'walk in the park.' It is not as simple as just having the Holy Spirit. The Holy Spirit must be used precisely, intelligently, and definitively, like a scalpel. This activity must begin by putting the flesh to death daily. Again, we must become familiar with the equipment God has given us and become strategically efficient in using it.

I protest by your rejoicing which I have in Christ Jesus
our Lord, I die daily. (1 Corinthians 15:31 KJV)

I beseech you therefore, brethren, by the mercies of
God, that ye present your bodies a living sacrifice,
holy, acceptable unto God, which is your
reasonable service. And be not conformed to this
world: but be ye transformed by the renewing of
your mind, that ye may prove what is that good,
and acceptable, and perfect, will of God. (Romans
12:1,2 KJV)

Before we go any further, I think it's important to note that God isn't doing this for us. He has given us power so that we can do what's necessary to overcome the enemy. So many I come across that pray to God to do this and do that. God has already done everything he's going to do. Now that we have the same power that Jesus had, God expects us to use that power to overcome the enemy of our flesh.

Here are a few examples of what we can do to overcome the enemy of our flesh.

> *Let not your heart be troubled: ye believe in God,*
> *believe also in me. (John 14:1 KJV)*

Friends, with so many issues in life that come to steal our peace, it is our responsibility to guard our peace. Let not your heart be troubled is an action that we must take to guard our hearts. And we do that by believing in God no matter the circumstance. The scripture says Abraham believed even against hope.

> *Who against hope believed in hope, that he might*
> *become the father of many nations; according to*
> *that which was spoken, So shall thy seed be.*
> *(Romans 4:18 KJV)*

Sometimes you just have to believe regardless of what you feel, see, or think. You just believe. This is how you keep your heart from being troubled.

Here's another responsibility of ours as it relates to this internal conflict.

> *Casting down imaginations, and every high thing that*
> *exalteth itself against the knowledge of God, and*
> *bringing into captivity every thought to the*
> *obedience of Christ; (2 Cor 10:5 KJV)*

I like the amplified version

> *We are destroying sophisticated arguments and every*
> *exalted and proud thing that sets itself up against*
> *the [true] knowledge of God, and we are taking*

every thought and purpose captive to the
obedience of Christ, (2 Cor 10:5 AMP)

Sophisticated arguments such as "you've tried that and it didn't work, you should just quit.

Gospel—I can do all things through Christ which strengthens me.

Sophisticated argument—I messed up. God is going to judge me.

Gospel—I messed up. I need to reconnect with God.

Sophisticated argument—I don't have what I need.

Gospel—Christ hath given us all things pertaining to life and godliness.

You must cast down those sophisticated false arguments in the mind and replace them with biblical truth.

Friends, when we realize God has given us power over the enemy and that Jesus' works have been completed. We understand the goal of God to raise sons and daughters who will do greater works.

Let's look at this one as well.

> *Wherefore seeing we also are compassed about with so*
> *great a cloud of witnesses, let us lay aside every*
> *weight, and the sin which doth so easily beset us,*
> *and let us run with patience the race that is set*
> *before us, (Hebrews 12:1 KJV)*

I like this NIV version as well.

> *Therefore, since we are surrounded by such a great*
> *cloud of witnesses, let us throw off everything that*
> *hinders and the sin that so easily entangles. And*

let us run with perseverance the race marked out
for us, (Hebrews 12:1 NIV)

Here we are again, and God is placing responsibility on us to lay aside every weight and sin. We don't need anyone to diagnose us. Most of us know precisely what hinders us from being our best selves, yet days, weeks, and years go by, allowing it. I've learned that God will not do what he has empowered and equipped us to do for ourselves. I call this self-deliverance. He doesn't, even when it gets hard and we cry and beg God to do it for us. Many of us are so familiar with the "do not instructions" of the Bible that we often overlook the "do instructions" or execute instructions of the Bible. It just makes sense to me. Why would God give us power and authority and do everything for us? That's like me buying you a 2023 fully loaded Bentley, and you call me the next day requesting a ride somewhere. I'm sure you understand how crazy that is. But that's likely how God feels when we ask God to do for us what he's equipped and empowered us to do for ourselves through the Holy Spirit.

Chapter 1

People Trouble

As we explore people trouble, let's first acknowledge Ephesians 6:12.

For we wrestle not against flesh and blood, but against principalities, against powers, against the rulers of the darkness of this world, against spiritual wickedness in high places.

People aren't our enemies, but spirits that oppress and influence them are. Throughout scripture, you will find several instances where different bible characters had to deal with people trouble. One, in particular, is the popular bible character Joseph. I won't assume that everyone reading this book is familiar with the story of Joseph. But Joseph, the 12th and most beloved son of Jacob, had to deal with people trouble. His brothers became jealous of him because of his favor with his father and his prophetic dreaming. The Bible tells us in Genesis 37 that the brothers plotted to kill him. Almost always, when you encounter people trouble, you can bet spirits of envy and jealousy are powering it. Listen, the mark of God's grace on your life will attract haters who will have disdain and contempt for you. Watch what the Bible says about envy.

*"But if ye have bitter envying and strife in your hearts,
glory not, and lie not against the truth. This
wisdom descendeth not from above, but is earthly,
sensual, devilish. For where envying and strife is,
there is confusion and every evil work." (James
3:14-16 KJV)*

Envy and strife are in every evil work. Whenever you're dealing with people, you understand the enemy is the master of confusion. It was Satan's envy toward God that caused him to try overthrowing heaven. Look at what the Bible says in Isaiah 14:12-15.

*How art thou fallen from heaven, O Lucifer, son of the
morning! How art thou cut down to the ground,
which didst weaken the nations! For thou hast said
in thine heart, I will ascend into heaven, I will
exalt my throne above the stars of God: I will sit
also upon the mount of the congregation, in the
sides of the north: I will ascend above the heights
of the clouds; I will be like the most High. Yet thou
shalt be brought down to hell, to the sides of
the pit.*

As Satan is the father of lies, he's also the father of envy and jealousy. Even Jesus engaged with envy and jealousy. The Pharisees and Saducees were constantly trying to discredit Jesus and eventually were the ones who gave Jesus up to the Romans.

*So when the crowd had assembled, Pilate asked them,
"Which one do you want me to release to you:
Barabbas, or Jesus who is called Christ?" For he
knew it was out of envy that they had handed
Jesus over to him. (Matthew 27:17-18)*

You know that if Jesus engaged with people trouble, you will too. But there's one common response between Joseph and Jesus. Although both dealt with people trouble through envy and jealousy, they both also never stopped doing what caused envy and jealousy to arise against them. So the correct response to envy and jealousy is to keep going and go even harder.

In order to do this, you will need to activate some Kingdom Equipment. Specifically, long-suffering and forgiveness. If you're gonna fulfill your purpose in life, you're gonna have to suffer awhile. And particularly suffering for and with the ones you're called to serve. Peter says it like this.

> *But the God of all grace, who hath called us unto his*
> *eternal glory by Christ Jesus, after that ye have*
> *suffered a while, make you perfect, stablish,*
> *strengthen, settle* you. (*1 Peter 5:10 KJV*)

You will need to activate forgiveness as well. Anytime you're dealing with people for any length of time, forgiveness will be a necessary ingredient to the relationship.

> *Then Peter came to Him and said, "Lord, how often*
> *shall my brother sin against me, and I forgive him?*
> *Up to seven times?"*
> *Jesus said to him, "I do not say to you, up to seven*
> *times, but up to seventy times seven. (Matthew*
> *18:21, 22 KJV)*

When Jesus came on the scene, it was the same people he was sent to serve that brought him before Pilate to be crucified. After all the healing, deliverance, feeding, and loving he did, they still betrayed him and gave him up to the Romans to be crucified. But Jesus understood one thing, and that was that he couldn't finish his assignment with unforgiveness in his heart. Yes, he was God, but he was all human as well. So he gets his heart right before the last part of his assignment.

Friends, you too will have to deal with people that will cause you emotional damage and heartache. Many times, the very ones you help are the ones who betray you. So, like your elder brother, forgiveness will be the order of the day. Learn to forgive it will make the weight of your assignment easier to bear.

Chapter 2

Personal Principle Trouble

Another trouble we could experience is personal principle trouble. Personal principle can be defined as a personal or specific basis of conduct or management. We all have personal principles. We all have specific reasons we conduct ourselves in a certain manner. Though our reasons vary, they are the foundation for our conduct and behavior.

The three Hebrew boys' commitment to bowing to no other gods was their principal personal trouble. It's a familiar story of how the king tried to force them to bow to his images of worship. Yet the Hebrews boys, understanding their decision's consequences, stood firm on their principle and did not bow. This act of civil disobedience put the Hebrew boys in great trouble and could have cost them their lives. May I ask? Is there anything in your life you believe in so much that you'll look death in the face for it? Yea, that's what these young men did. As great as that is, we're not finished bragging about these young men. What do you do when you're in trouble because of your beliefs and principles? How do you respond to the consequences of trouble? A part of recognizing what kind of trouble you're in is also understanding what your response should be. This response had to be different here. The Hebrew boys were facing principalities and powers. This wasn't jealousy and envy. This was power and control on another level. Nothing they could have said or done could or would have changed their situation. So what did they do? The Bible says while in the fiery furnace; they walked around in the midst of the fire. The Bible says that the king saw a fourth man in the fire with them, and the form of the fourth man is like the Son of God. The only explanation we have for this is that the three Hebrew boys activated this scripture.

> *But thou art holy, O thou that inhabitest the praises of*
> *Israel. (Psalms 22:3)*

Praise is the key to bringing God into a situation. The Bible doesn't specifically say that they were praising God. It refers to them walking around. But praise has various looks and styles. Whatever they were doing, it brought God into the fiery furnace with them and they remained unburned, unharmed, nor was a hair of their head singed, neither were their coats changed, nor the smell of fire on them. Listen, if you're in a situation that only God can deal with because you stood on what you believe. Praise God and wait on him to get involved in your situation with you. God can't resist praise. He'll show up every time.

Chapter 3

Demonic Resistance Trouble

Friends, one of the best ways to know if you're experiencing demonic resistance is when you're doing something that you know is the will of God for your life and the resistance to that assignment becomes intense beyond normal circumstances. It seems the enemy throws everything at you, to include the kitchen sink. You've prayed, fasted, and put to work to your faith, but it seems the breakthrough is nowhere in sight. If you are or ever have experienced this, you may have experienced demonic resistance trouble. In the book of Daniel, we find Daniel doing all the right things and, most of all, praying to God three times a day. We all know prayer is the will of God. We know that prayer is the avenue through which we bring heavenly things into the earth realm. But there are times even when we pray we experience demonic resistance.

The Bible tells us in Daniel 6 that the presidents and princes sought to find fault against Daniel but couldn't find anything. So they went after something that would cause him to oppose his God. This demonic resistance trouble combines people trouble, principalities and powers, and demonic resistance. The people trouble came from the presidents and princes who sought to find fault against Daniel. The principalities and powers were the king's decree. No one except King Darius could ask for a petition from any God or man for thirty days.

Because of this decree and Daniel's commitment to God, Daniel ends up in the lion's den. But God sent an angel to shut the mouths of the lions. So Daniel was rescued from the lion's den, and the king throws those who set Daniel up into the lion's den.

That was just the preliminary issue while Daniel was awaiting an answer to his prayer. Then, finally, in Daniel chapter 10, he has a vision, and an angel comes to him saying from the first day Daniel prayed, God heard him. But the prince of Persia, a demonic force, withstood the angel from coming so much that one of the chief angels, Michael, came to help him.

Many of us are unfamiliar with the angelic and demonic realm, but make no mistake; angels and demons exist. So the scripture says in Psalms 91:11, For he shall give his angels charge over thee, to keep thee in all thy ways. Every believer has angels assigned to them, and these angels play a special part in our lives. Hebrews 1:14 says, Are they not all ministering spirits, sent forth to minister for them who shall be heirs of salvation? I often say that a portion of angels are the transportation department of the Kingdom. Their job is to bring what heaven has for us into manifestation on earth. Angels do various things for us, including assisting in spiritual battles.

> Bless the LORD, ye his angels, that excel in strength,
>   that do his commandments, hearkening unto the
>   voice of his word.
> Bless ye the LORD, all ye his hosts; ye ministers of his,
>   that do his pleasure. (Psalms 103:20, 21)

The word hosts in the Greek is tsaba tsebaah means a mass or army of organized angels that go out to war.

> *And suddenly there was with the angel a multitude of the heavenly host praising God and saying: (Luke 2:13)*

When angels come, they come ready to do battle and wage war on your behalf. Therefore, you must become familiar with engaging, commanding, and hearing from them.

> *And it came to pass that night, that the angel of the LORD went out, and smote in the camp of the Assyrians an hundred fourscore and five thousand: and when they arose early in the morning, behold, they were all dead corpses (2 Kings 19:35)*

You must employ angelic hosts when facing principalities, powers, and spiritual wickedness in high places. Many don't believe in angels, but I'm of the conviction that if I'm going to believe the Bible, I'm going to believe the whole Bible. If you're experiencing demonic resistance, you need to employ your angels and possibly for angelic assistance. But whatever you do, don't stop praying. I've found that praying in the spirit also helps with demonic resistance. When you don't know what else to pray for, the spirit takes over and makes intercession for us with groanings that cannot be uttered. But know this you can't be more than a conqueror if there's never anything to conquer. Romans 8:37 says, "Nay, in all these things we are more than conquerors through him that loved us." If only we knew the full extent of God's love. His love is before us, with us, and proceeds with us to ensure that we have access to all he planned for us. The Bible doesn't say the weapon won't form; it says it won't prosper.

Chapter 4

Bad Trouble, God Allowed

When you mention God and trouble in the same sentence, many people don't understand the connection and get confused about God's love for them. Let me be clear: God's love for you can never be questioned. God is love, and you can't experience genuine love without him. But yes, sometimes God and trouble are connected, and God can seem to be the cause.

Let's take Job as an example. The Bible says he was perfect and upright, feared God, and eschewed evil. Job was very well esteemed among his children and his family. Yet trouble came to his house. And according to the scriptures, God allowed it. Not only did God allow it, but he started it. Now let's look at this according to the scriptures.

> *Now there was a day when the sons of God came to present themselves before the LORD, and Satan came also among them. And the LORD said unto Satan, Whence comest thou? Then Satan answered the LORD, and said, From going to and*

fro in the earth, and from walking up and down in it. And the LORD said unto Satan, Hast thou considered my servant Job, that there is none like him in the earth, a perfect and an upright man, one that feareth God, and escheweth evil? Then Satan answered the LORD, and said, Doth Job fear God for nought? Hast not thou made an hedge about him, and about his house, and about all that he hath on every side? thou hast blessed the work of his hands, and his substance is increased in the land. But put forth thine hand now, and touch all that he hath, and he will curse thee to thy face. And the LORD said unto Satan, Behold, all that he hath is in thy power; only upon himself put not forth thine hand. So Satan went forth from the presence of the LORD. (Job 1:6-12)

Now let us ask ourselves, was God testing Job? Was God punishing Job? Or was God proving something to Satan? The answer is very simple. God was proving something to Satan. God knew Job's love and commitment to him, so he allowed Satan to afflict him but not take his life. Bad trouble God allowed. So what does Job do when encountering this trouble? On one end, Job initially responds in vs 20 of chapter 1.

Then Job arose, and rent his mantle, and shaved his head, and fell down upon the ground, and worshipped, And said, Naked came I out of my mother's womb, and naked shall I return thither: the LORD gave, and the LORD hath taken away; blessed be the name of the LORD. In all this Job sinned not, nor charged God foolishly. (Job 1:20-22)

Then the Bible intentionally emphasizes that Job didn't sin or charge God foolishly. Friends, we must be careful how we respond to trouble so we don't falsely and ignorantly charge God foolishly. It would be easy to charge God as testing or punishing Job without knowing God's intent and purposes. Here are some scriptures to keep in mind.

> *Nay but, O man, who art thou that repliest against*
> *God? Shall the thing formed say to him that*
> *formed it, Why hast thou made me thus? (Romans*
> *9:20)*

> *People ruin their lives by their own foolishness and*
> *then are angry at the LORD. (Proverbs 19:3 NLT)*

> *My brethren, count it all joy when ye fall into divers*
> *temptations; Knowing this, that the trying of your*
> *faith worketh patience. But let patience*
> *have her perfect work, that ye may be perfect and*
> *entire, wanting nothing. (James 1:2-4)*

> *Be not rash with thy mouth, and let not thine heart be*
> *hasty to utter any thing before God: for God is in*
> *heaven, and thou upon earth: therefore let thy*
> *words be few. (Ecclesiastes 5:2)*

Friends, regardless of the circumstances, how you feel, and what is out of order, please don't alienate the person who can help you. Many times, he's the only one that can help you. Watch your tongue, hold your peace, remember God's love for you, cry out to God for help, and he will hear you.

One of the worst things you can do when trouble comes is get angry with God. That's why I often teach that one of the first things a believer must learn after accepting Christ is the revelation of God's love. You must have unwavering confidence in the love of God. Not just a general love for the world and mankind. But a specific love for you.

But then Job complains in Job 7. And let me tell you, God's response is something I don't think Job was ready for. So here is just a tiny portion of God's response in Job 38.

> *Then the LORD answered Job out of the whirlwind and said: "Who is this who obscures My counsel by words without knowledge? Now brace yourself like a man; I will question you, and you shall inform e. Where were you when I laid the foundations of the earth? Tell Me, if you have understanding. Who fixed its measurements? Surely you know! Or who stretched a measuring line across it? On what were its foundations set, or who laid its cornerstone, while the morning stars sang together and all the sons of God shouted for joy? Who enclosed the sea behind doors when it burst forth from the womb, when I made the clouds its garment and thick darkness its blanket when I fixed its boundaries and set in place its bars and doors, and I declared: 'You may come this far, but no farther; here your proud waves must stop'? In your days, have you commanded the morning or assigned the dawn its place, that it might spread to the ends of the earth and shake the wicked out of it? The earth takes shape like clay under a seal; its hills stand out like the folds of a garment. Light is withheld from the wicked, and their upraised arm is broken." (Job 38:1-15 Berean Study Bible)*

If I got a response from God like that, I would immediately apologize and get some act right real quick, lol. I believe Job did just that. When Job prays for his friends, it seems there was no clap back.

Friends, sometimes we never know how long our trouble may last. But don't get too relaxed in your trouble. God is a deliverer. It's in his nature to always rescue his people out of their trouble. But that doesn't always mean that he'll come right away. Sometimes there are lessons to be learned from our trouble. And other times, God sets a time for our deliverance. But we've seen consistently that sometimes God will require us to take part in that deliverance.

Job's willingness to forgive his friends activated his deliverance and restoration. We discuss forgiveness all the time and discuss it as if it's easy to do. Forgiveness is difficult to do. Forgiveness often involves emotional trauma that torments the soul. To forgive, one must know that forgiveness is necessary, decide to forgive with their will, and operate emotional intelligence to overcome the tormenting and reoccurring feelings. It is an actual act of absolute obedience to God. Sometimes saying I don't want to forgive, but I want my healing more than I want to keep this offense.

Chapter 5

Bad Trouble, God Allowed
(Part 2)

So many times when we find ourselves in trouble, our first prayer to God is to get us out of this. It's often an automatic response to resort to self-preservation immediately. Self-preservation can be a sin. It's an element of pride that says to God that we don't need him.

Trouble is a part of our human experience. No one escapes it, dodges it, or outruns it.

> *Man that is born of a woman is of few days, and full of trouble. (Job 14:1)*

> *Behold, the hour cometh, yea, is now come, that ye shall be scattered, every man to his own, and shall leave me alone: and yet I am not alone, because the father is with me. These things I have spoken unto you, that in me ye might have peace. In the world ye shall have tribulation: but be of good cheer; I have overcome the world. (John 16:32, 33)*

We've got to learn how to respond to trouble. Sometimes the severity of our trouble can depend on how we respond. But then again, sometimes it doesn't matter whether or not we like the trouble. Whether or not we respond appropriately. Sometimes our trouble has a purpose and is intentional. Sometimes our trouble can be initiated by God.

> *Thus saith the LORD of hosts, the God of Israel, unto all that are carried away captives, whom I have caused to be carried away from Jerusalem unto Babylon; Build ye houses, and dwell in them; and plant gardens, and eat the fruit of them; Take ye wives, and beget sons and daughters; and take wives for your sons, and give your daughters to husbands, that they may bear sons and daughters; that ye may be increased there, and not diminished. And seek the peace of the city whither I have caused you to be carried away captives and pray unto the LORD for it: for in the peace thereof shall ye have peace. For thus saith the LORD of hosts, the God of Israel; Let not your prophets and your diviners, that be in the midst of you, deceive you, neither hearken to your dreams which ye cause to be dreamed. For they prophesy falsely unto you in my name: I have not sent them, saith the LORD. For thus saith the LORD, That after seventy years be accomplished at Babylon I will visit you, and perform my good word toward you, in causing you to return to this place. For I know the thoughts that I think toward you, saith the LORD, thoughts of peace, and not of evil, to give you an expected end. (Jeremiah 29:4-11)*

Many are only familiar with vs. 11 of this chapter. Of course, we love the scriptures that speak of the wonderful things God has planned for us. But we should read more about the context of these scriptures to understand how these things come about.

Notice in vs. 4 that God put the children of Israel in captivity. Have you ever wondered about some situations you've been in? Have you ever thought that some situations you've been caught up in were the punishment of God? How do we know when we're dealing with the consequences of our actions?

One thing I've learned in my journey is that when you find yourself in a situation you or others can get you out of, this trouble could be initiated by God or a consequence of an action. Either way, only God can fix the situation.

Notice the instructions God gives through the prophet concerning this trouble. First, build houses, dwell in them, plant gardens, and eat the fruit of them. Take wives and have children. Increase in number while in captivity. Then he instructs them to activate peace and pray for the city where they are being held captive. This is very important. But let's understand why before we dive into activating peace.

The prophet continues by warning them about listening to false prophets who deceived them and being deceived by their dreams. The truth about their captivity is that they will be there for 70 years.

> *We often sing the song "Trouble don't last always."*
> *It's a song that helps us through trying times and*
> *speaks to the fact that what we're currently*
> *experiencing will end one day. The scripture says,*
> *"To everything there is a season, and a time to*
> *every purpose under the heaven." (Ecclesiastes*
> *3:1)*

Friends, you need to know that trouble doesn't last always, and this current trouble will be no different. But when the trouble is started or allowed by God, it usually lasts a little while. The most famous captivity other than this Babylonian captivity was the 400-year Egyptian captivity that God initiated.

Therefore, activating peace is a vital part of the instructions given by the prophet Jeremiah. Different trouble calls for different responses, but peace is necessary for long-term trouble.

> *These things I have spoken unto you, that in me ye might have peace. In the world ye shall have tribulation: but be of good cheer; I have overcome the world. (John 16:33)*

> *Be careful for nothing; but in every thing by prayer and supplication with thanksgiving let your requests be made known unto God. And the peace of God, which passeth all understanding, shall keep your hearts and minds through Christ Jesus. (Philippians 4:6,7 KJV)*

> *Be anxious for nothing, but in everything by prayer and supplication, with thanksgiving, let your requests be made known to God; and the peace of God, which surpasses all understanding, will guard your hearts and minds through Christ Jesus. (Philippians 4:6,7 NKJV)*

> *Do not be anxious about anything, but in everything by prayer and supplication with thanksgiving let your requests be made known to God. And the peace of God, which surpasses all understanding, will guard your hearts and*

> *your minds in Christ Jesus. (Philippians*
> *4:6,7 ESV)*

With these three versions, I would like to submit that the prescription for anxiety is prayer and thanksgiving, which also activates the peace of God. But, on the other hand, anxiety is the opposite of peace. According to Oxford languages, anxiety is a feeling of worry, nervousness, or unease, typically about an imminent event or something with an uncertain outcome.

For many, the issue is that they know they're thinking is being affected by anxiety but feel helpless to deal with it. Let these scriptures encourage you.

> *You will keep him in perfect*
> *peace, whose mind is stayed on You, Because he*
> *trusts in You. (Isaiah 26:3 NKJV)*

Notice that you have to keep your mind on God for this peace to be activated.

> *Now the Lord of peace himself give you peace always*
> *by all means. The Lord be with you all. (2*
> *Thessalonians 3:16 KJV)*

Peace is always available to you. Peace is not outside of you; it's inside of you. Peace is a part of the fruit of the spirit.

To pray for peace as if it's something outside your control to activate is an insult to God. Peace is a part of your Kingdom equipment for life and godliness.

Let's talk more about activating peace.

> *And let the peace of God rule in your hearts, to the*

> *which also ye are called in one body; and be ye*
> *thankful. (Colossians 3:15 KJV)*

Peace is not just going to activate automatically. Activate it and let it do what it does. You've got to recognize when your thinking is not being guided by peace and activate it. This is the second time we've seen a connection between peace and thanksgiving.

Here are some other scriptures:

> *And let the peace of God rule in your hearts, to the*
> *which also ye are called in one body; and be ye*
> *thankful. (Colossians 3:15 KJV)*

> *And he repaired the altar of the LORD, and sacrificed*
> *thereon peace offerings and thank offerings, and*
> *commanded Judah to serve the LORD God of*
> *Israel. (2 Chronicles 33:16 KJV)*

Most Peace offerings in the Old Testament were also brought with Thanksgiving offerings.

> *Besides the cakes, he shall offer for his offering*
> *leavened bread with the sacrifice of thanksgiving*
> *of his peace offerings. (Leviticus 7:13 KJV)*

Friends, as you can see, thanksgiving is a necessary part of activating peace in your life. Especially when dealing with trouble that only God can get you out of.

> *The LORD shall fight for you, and ye shall hold your*
> *peace. (Exodus 14:14 KJV)*

Friends, you must activate peace if you want God to fight for you. Activating peace is not God's Job; it's ours. Peace is not outside ourselves, but within, through the fruit of the spirit.

> *Finally, brothers, whatever is true, whatever is honorable, whatever is right, whatever is pure, whatever is lovely, whatever is admirable—if anything is excellent or praiseworthy—think on these things. Whatever you have learned or received or heard from me, or seen in me, put it into practice. And the God of peace will be with you. (Philippians 4:8,9 KJV)*

Again, I can't stress this enough. Peace is a part of the fruit of the spirit. It is activated by prayer, thanksgiving, and controlling our thought life.

Chapter 6

Good Trouble

John Lewis became famous for the quote, "Good trouble." He called it necessary trouble. What a statement, quote, and call to action from one of our time's most significant civil rights activists and congressmen. I'm unsure if he meant any biblical connection to his statement. Still, there is a biblical context for good trouble.

The first person who comes to mind is Moses. You know the story of Moses. Moses grew up as an Egyptian child in the house of Pharoah, the King of Egypt, alongside his brother, brought in by an adoptive mother, Pharoah's daughter, who then hires his actual birth mother, a Hebrew slave, to care for him as his nanny. Now I know that was a lot to take in and grasp, but it's an accurate description of the beginning of Moses' life. I can't go into all of that in this book. Still, I believe that Moses' mother instilled in Moses some Hebrew mindsets and customs that messed with Moses' identity while growing up. Sometimes we never know why or how life contributes to people's decisions. However, my prophetic imagination believes that Mom Moses was planting seeds that Moses had to come to grips with, eventually. And this is where Moses comes to a crossroads as he begins adulthood. He recognizes who he is, and the struggle with his reality causes him to make a decision that would change his whole life. You know the story Moses, a young prince who grew up in royalty, angrily takes the life of an Egyptian guard who was beating a fellow Hebrew slave. This anger outburst caused Moses to run into exile because, though he was a prince, he recognized who he was and knew he would be relegated and punished for his actions. Moses then spends 40 years in exile away from his mother and those he grew up knowing as family. But while in exile, he finds a family of his own.

The interesting thing about the situation with Moses is that I'm sure Moses had no clue about the prophecy on his life before he was even born. What prophecy, do you ask? The word that was spoken to Abraham was that his people would be captives for 400 years. And here comes Moses right around that 400-year mark. God calls Moses from a burning bush to return to Egypt, where he is likely on the most wanted list, to tell Pharoah to let the Hebrew people go. The Hebrew people, likely after 400 years, had lost hope and grew weary of crying and praying. But I'm so glad that God never forgets. He never leaves us or forsakes us. And one thing I've learned about God is that he continually raises a deliverer from among us. Moses going to Pharoah to deliver this message was good trouble. It took courage to return to Egypt and even more courage to make these demands to Pharoah. Good trouble is not for the faint of heart. This mission was to be no walk in the park. When Pharoah initially rejects Moses, from there, things go from bad to worse. For deliverers, this is nothing new. Good trouble is never easy, as delivering the Hebrew people out of Egypt wasn't easy. Neither was getting them into the promised land. Joshua and Caleb led them into the promised land and were immediately met with significant resistance. They, even at one point, faced battles against a gang of other nations coming against them at one time.

And Joshua said unto the children of Israel, Come
hither, and hear the words of the LORD your

> *God. And Joshua said, Hereby ye shall know that*
> *the living God is among you, and that he will*
> *without fail drive out from before you the*
> *Canaanites, and the Hittites, and the Hivites,*
> *and the Perizzites, and the Girgashites, and the*
> *Amorites, and the Jebusites. (Joshua 3:9,*
> *10 KJV)*

When the children of Israel approached the promised land, God spoke to them about what they could expect in this land. They already knew it was a prosperous land, a land flowing with milk and honey. So the miracles of the wilderness they knew they wouldn't need anymore. But what they didn't know was that someone was occupying the land God had promised them. Someone was maintaining their land for them until they arrived. These -ites verse 10 speaks about are the Canaanites, Hittites, Hivites, Perrizites, Girgashites, Amorites, and Jebusites, which represent the seven spirits we all must fight in our land (the flesh).

Canaanite Spirit (H3667)–Spirit of greed and lust for the accumulation of earthly and material wealth. Merchants who humiliate by great wealth; Financial giants;

Hittite Spirit (H2850)–Spirit that brings fear, confusion, and discouragement; sons of terror. The word terror refers to an extreme manifestation of fear.

Hivite Spirit (H2340) (H2333) (H2332)–life giving, living place; This spirit claims to offer a good lifestyle outside of God. Philosophers and motivation speakers operate in this spirit a lot.

Perrizite Spirit (H6522) (H6519) (H6518)–rural dweller, open region, unwalled village. This spirit lives in isolation and has trouble maintaining relationships. It causes people to separate themselves and live unprotected lives.

Girgashite Spirit (H1622)–clay dwellers referring to people who are earthly. Guided by reasoning and logic. Backsliders with unstable mindsets.

Amorite Spirit (H567)–A sayer, arrogant and boastful in speech. Fault finders who operate in pride.

Jebusite Spirit (H2983)–means to trodden down; to put down and humiliate others. Believe that certain people are inherently inferior.

These spirits were in the land of promise that the children of Israel had to defeat if they wanted to live in peace. This was good trouble. The trouble of self development. The trouble of facing the enemy in a me.

Friends, good trouble is when you're chasing the enemy, not the enemy chasing you. Whether it be in deliverance, getting others out of captivity or inheritance, claiming the inheritance of God's promises, good trouble is tough, but always worth all the spoils you will gain.

As we come to a close of this book, I want to equip the body of Christ to appropriately deal with the troubles of life and life as a believer with a real enemy. The scripture says, "Man that is born of a woman is of few days, and full of trouble." (Job 14:1). I can't think of a year when I didn't face one of these six troubles. But I also understand that I didn't know the secrets to deal with these troubles either. I realize that trouble doesn't last always, and that God is a deliverer in his own time. But I believe there are rewards for dealing with the trouble. Let me explain.

Let's take Joseph, for example, dealing with people trouble. What if Joseph had stopped dreaming and interpreting dreams? What if he had just taken his gift and hid it from the world? What if he had gotten lazy and depressed and stopped operating in the spirit of excellence? The answer to these questions would significantly impact Joseph's journey and destiny. His spirit of excellence caused him to be promoted everywhere he went. And his prophetic gift in the area of dreaming and dream interpretation opened the door for him with Pharoah.

What about the children of Israel in Babylonian captivity who had been instructed to operate in peace and marry and have children? Marriage and having children would have been a disaster without operating in peace.

The three Hebrew boys praising God while in the fire brought God into the fire with them. Therefore, the scripture says he dwells in the midst of praises.

> *But thou art holy, O thou that inhabitest the praises of*
> *Israel. (Psalms 22:3 KJV)*

Friends, how you handle trouble is essential. That's why God has given all these examples as prescriptions for when we find ourselves in the troubles of life. God will not always come and rescue us right away. Instead, we must use the equipment he's given us through his word to deal with the troubles of life. Trouble doesn't have to dominate you when you know how to identify your trouble, listen to God, and use your tools.

Chapter 7

A Few Biblical Prescriptions to Use

Fear–Love

Love is the Kingdom's prescription for fear.

> There is no fear in love; <u>but perfect love casteth out
> fear</u>: because fear hath torment. He that feareth is
> not made perfect in love. (1 John 4:18 KJV)

Mourning/Grief–Joy

Joy is the Kingdom's prescription for grief.

> To appoint unto them that mourn in Zion, to give unto
> them beauty for ashes, <u>the oil of joy for mourning</u>,
> the garment of praise for the spirit of heaviness;
> that they might be called trees of righteousness, the
> planting of the LORD, that he might be glorified.
> (Isaiah 61:3 KJV)

Spirit of heaviness/depression—Praise

Praise is the Kingdom's prescription for the spirit of heaviness/depression

> *To appoint unto them that mourn in Zion, to give unto*
> *them beauty for ashes, the oil of joy for mourning,*
> *<u>the garment of praise for the spirit of heaviness</u>;*
> *that they might be called trees of righteousness, the*
> *planting of the LORD, that he might be glorified.*
> *(Isaiah 61:3 KJV)*

Anxiety—Peace

Peace is the Kingdom's prescription for anxiety.

Be anxious for nothing, but in everything by prayer and supplication, with thanksgiving, let your requests be made known to God; And the peace of God, which passeth all understanding, shall keep your hearts and minds through Christ Jesus.

Peace is activated by prayer and thanksgiving.

Pride—Humility

Humility is the Kingdom's prescription for pride.

> *But he giveth more grace. Wherefore he saith, God*
> *resisteth the proud, but giveth grace unto the*
> *humble. (James 4:6 KJV)*

I like the way the NIV version says it.

> *But he gives us more grace. That is why scripture says:*

"God opposes the proud but shows favor to the humble." (James 4:6 NIV)

These are just a few examples. Throughout the scriptures, God has instructed us to deal with some issues we face in this life. I pray this book has blessed you and opened your eyes to the Kingdom equipment God has given us to handle the cares of this life. We realize that it's important how we go through the trials of life. Most of the time, God isn't coming to get us out right away, but while we await deliverance, he empowers us to overcome.

About the Author

Apostle Terry Stephens II is a powerful apostolic and prophetic leader used by God to usher in a fresh perspective concerning Kingdom government and leadership to bring the body of Christ together for the last days' stand. He operates with a unique revelatory anointing that focuses on breaking the chains of religion and tradition.

With a military perspective, Apostle Stephens is passionate about fivefold ministry leadership with a kingdom agenda. While serving in the United States Army and deployed to Iraq, God gave Apostle Stephens the vision of Truth & Wholeness Ministries. Led by the Spirit of God, Truth & Wholeness Ministries is to resemble the Army through cultural diversity, developing leaders, and establishing a distinct kingdom culture.

Truth & Wholeness Ministries was birthed in June 2011 and continues to grow and expand its territory. Apostle Stephens has a heart for the prodigal sons of the Kingdom and is committed to bringing the restoration message to all hearers. Apostle Stephens is a Network of Local Churches (NLC) member established by Apostle Lafayette Scales of Rhema Christian Center in Columbus, Ohio. He founded T & W Publishing and is the author of Jesus Our Fivefold Ministry Leader, released in March 2012.

Other books & manuals he has written include Kingdom Equipment and God's Business Plan. Apostle Stephens is passionate about kingdom leadership and team ministry and committed to bringing excellence in leadership to the body of Christ.

In 2015, Apostle Stephens founded Dad Leadership Group, a coaching, consulting, and leadership development small business to help develop leaders and enhance community-based organizations, churches, and leaders at all levels. Then, in 2016, Apostle Stephens was led by God to change the name of Truth & Wholeness Ministries to Manifestation Church—training sons and daughters in the manifestation of sonship.

Soon after, in 2020, he and his wife, Janet Stephens, launched the non-profit Bridges to Life Community Services, serving the urban community, building families, and connecting resources. As a military man of 25 years, Apostle Stephens refers to his calling as a spiritual boot camp where he births kingdom citizens, equips them to achieve wholeness, then sends them for kingdom advancement.

Apostle Stephens, with his wife, Lady Janet Stephens, and their blended family of six children, Janeyce, Janique, Tre, Jaylin, Andre, and Maya, is on a mission to see all men realize the abundant life our Jesus came to give.

facebook.com/apostletw
twitter.com/apostletw8
instagram.com/apostletw

Also by Terry Stephens

Kingdom Equipment 101: Tools for Kingdom Purpose

God's Business Plan

www.ingramcontent.com/pod-product-compliance
Lightning Source LLC
Chambersburg PA
CBHW070946120626
46546CB00004B/1588